The Pearl of Portsmouth

A Story of Dr. Martin Luther King, Jr.

written by

Tammi J. Truax

illustrated by

Rev. Lillian Buckley

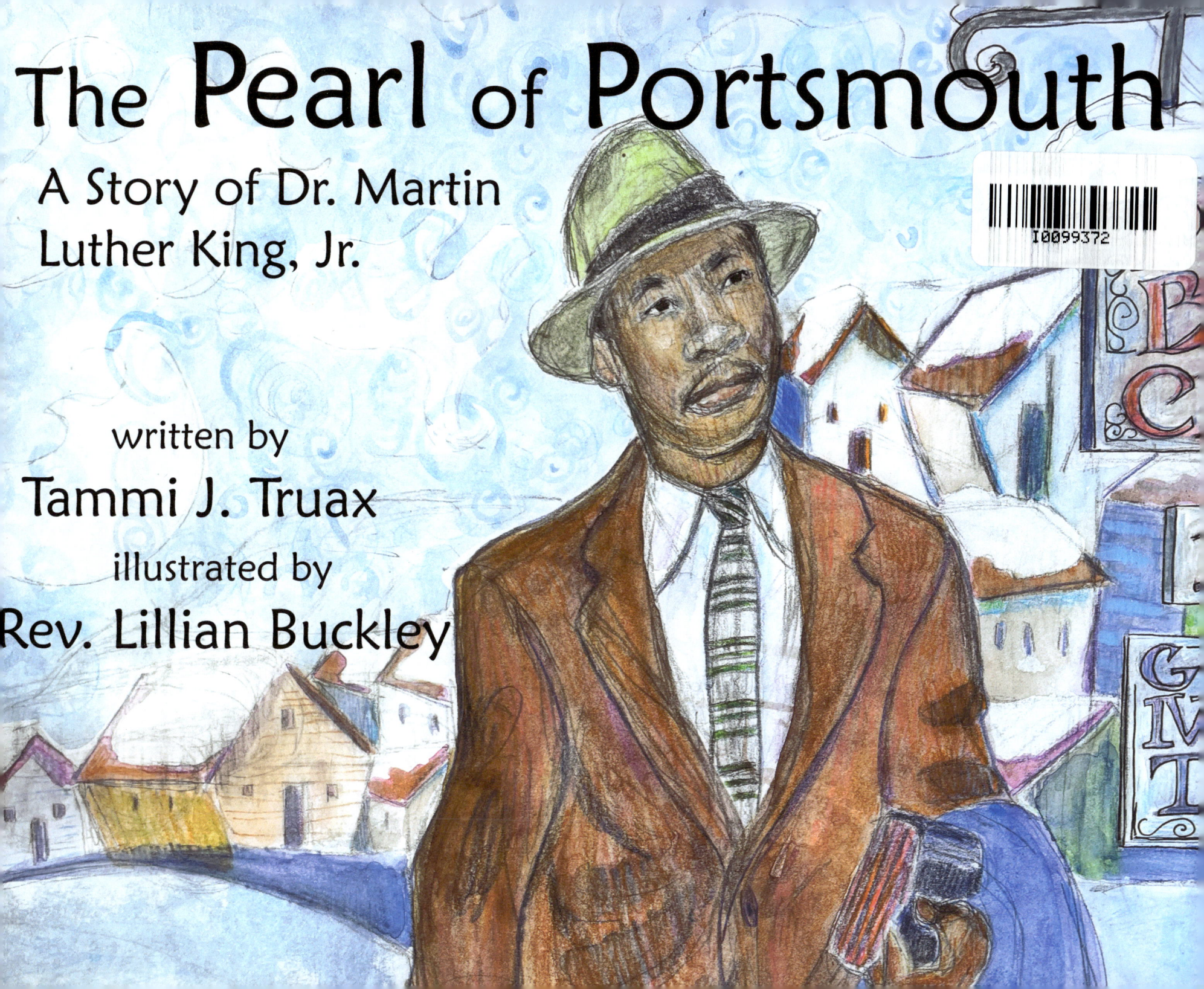

Publisher's Cataloguing-in-Publication Data

Names: Truax, Tammi J., author. Buckley, Lillian, illustrator.
Title: The Pearl of Portsmouth
Subtitle: A Story of Dr. Martin Luther King, Jr.
Description: first edition, paperback, NH: Piscataqua Press, [2022].
Summary: "An introduction to Dr. King's life and work, focused on his 1952 visit to Portsmouth, NH."--Provided by publisher.
ISBN: 978-1-958669-06-8
Subjects: JUVENILE NONFICTION / King, Martin Luther, Jr., 1929-1968 / American history / Civil Rights Movement / New Hampshire
Classification: DDC 323.092 [B]

For the children of Portsmouth and beyond:
Learn from our history now, so that you may help make a history that you and your children will be proud to share someday.

- T.T.

For the former first lady of People's Baptist Church, the late Mrs. Margie Alexander Hailes. When I was a small, shy child she placed my hand in hers, teaching me to use my voice and the importance of me, a little black girl, in a world whose sounds would drown me out if I did not object. And for my Bates College Art Professor, the late Donald R. Lent who saw in my work the ability to tell a story.

- L.B.

There was a time, not so long ago, when American people were separated from each other because of the color of their skin.

There were separate neighborhoods, separate schools, separate stores, separate churches, separate sports, even separate drinking fountains, which were marked "white" and "colored".

This kind of unfair treatment of people is called segregation.

In the little seaside city of Portsmouth, New Hampshire there were several churches for white people to choose from, and one church for all people of color.

Though it was a separate church it was called The People's Baptist Church. It was located in the center of town on Pearl Street, and has since come to be called The Pearl.

On a cold autumn morning in 1952, a young guest preacher came to town to give a sermon at the Pearl. His name was Reverend Martin Luther King, Jr.

This is how he explained the problem,
"Men often hate each other because they fear each other,
They fear each other because they don't know each other,
They don't know each other because they cannot communicate;
They cannot communicate because they are separated."

That same Sunday morning a member of the visiting choir stood up and performed a beautiful solo. She and Reverend King were sweethearts. Her name was Miss Coretta Scott.

CONSIDER THE
LILIES OF THE FIELD
FATHER FORGIVE
THEY KNOW NOT

She sang,
"I am a poor pilgrim of sorrow.
I'm tossed in this wide world alone.
I've heard of a city called Heaven.
I've started to make it my home."

Reverend King and Miss Scott were married soon after. They lived in Boston until they earned college degrees, then moved to Alabama. They devoted their lives to ending the separation of the citizens of every state, to ending segregation in schools, stores, public buildings, on public transportation and in places of worship...

BOSTON
1951-1953

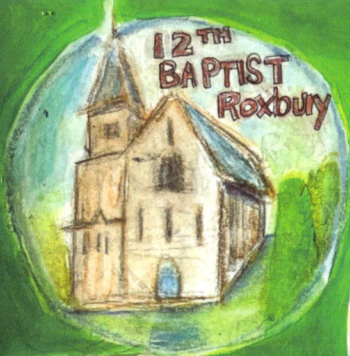

12TH BAPTIST Roxbury

DIPLOMA
• BOSTON UNIVERSITY
• NEW ENGLAND CONSERVATORY OF MUSIC

MEMPHIS
1968

I AM A MAN
I AM A MAN
I AM A MAN

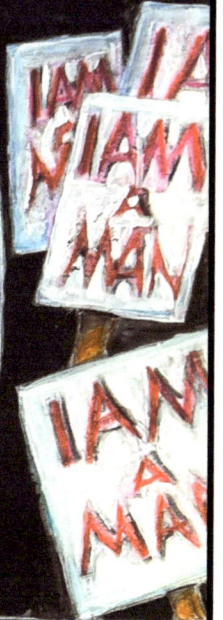

MONTGOMERY
1954-1960

BUS BOYCOTT 1955

"RIGHT HERE IN MONTGOMERY, WHEN THE HISTORY BOOKS ARE WRITTEN FOR THE FUTURE, SOMEBODY WILL HAVE TO SAY, 'THERE LIVED A RACE OF PEOPLE, A BLACK PEOPLE,... A PEOPLE WHO HAD THE MORAL COURAGE TO STAND UP FOR THEIR RIGHTS.'" -1955

0116

ATLANTA
1960

NOBEL PEACE PRIZE -1964

ALFR. NOBEL
NAT MDCCC XXXIII OB. MDCCC XCVI

"THE RICHER WE BECOME MATERIALLY THE POORER WE HAVE BECOME MORALLY AND SPIRITUALLY. WE HAVE LEARNED TO FLY THE AIR LIKE BIRDS AND SWIM THE SEA LIKE FISH, BUT WE HAVE NOT LEARNED THE SIMPLE ART OF LIVING TOGETHER AS BROTHERS" -1964

...so that one day Reverend King would implore the whole country,

"Let freedom ring
from the prodigious mountaintops
of New Hampshire."

FREEDOM

...Let it ring.
DR. MARTIN LUTHER KING JR
AUGUST 28, 1963

Let it ring.

Historical Notes

In 1952 Harry S. Truman was the President of the United States, though his term was winding down and election campaigns were in full swing and televised for the first time. The country was prospering according to many measurements. The *I Love Lucy* show was a big hit, the Mr. Potato Head toy had just been released, the average cost of a new house was $9,000. and Dr. Jonas Salk developed the polio vaccine.

Yet we were a very segregated nation, with segregation policies being legal all over the country. In the very first illustration in this book, Reverend Buckley included the words "separate but equal, 1896" referring to the 1896 Supreme Court case known as Plessy v. Ferguson which declared that segregation was constitutional. It would not be until the dawn of the American Civil rights Movement in 1954 that the separate but equal decision would be overturned by Brown v Board of Education. When writing the majority opinion case, Chief Justice Warren stated "the doctrine of 'separate but equal' has no place" in public education, calling segregated schools "inherently unequal," and declaring that the plaintiffs in the case were being "deprived of the equal protection of the laws guaranteed by the 14th Amendment."

Dr. King became the leader of the Civil Rights movement which lasted from 1954 to 1968, One of the most illustrious events of the movement took place on August 28, 1963 and is known as the March on Washington. More than 200,000 people of all races gathered peacefully in Washington, DC that day with the goal of pushing civil rights legislation forward and gaining job equality. The highlight of the march was Dr. King's speech in which he continually stated, "I have a dream…"

When Dr. King and Miss Scott visited Portsmouth, NH on October 26, 1952 he was a graduate student of theology at Boston University and was focused on his aspiring career as a minister. He was only 23 years old. Miss Scott was then a student at the New England Conservatory of Music. They had been dating most of the year, and married eight months later. They were invited to the People's Baptist Church for their 59th anniversary celebration. We know that the sermon he gave that day was titled "Going Forward by Going Backward" but the sermon itself was not preserved. In 1952 the enduring value of Reverend King's words was not fully appreciated, and his legacy and martyrdom, were unimaginable.

Author's notes

As a student and teacher of local history and as a writer, I've long been compelled to share the stories of our past, especially those that I've feared would be forgotten.

I was surprised when I learned that Dr. King had visited Portsmouth, New Hampshire, my home town, and had preached in a building that had been deteriorating for decades. It bothered me that I hadn't known, and that my children didn't know. I decided that I wanted to write a picture book so that children would know what is widely unknown in the region. I worked on the manuscript for years to gather all the known facts about Dr. and Mrs. King's visit. Unfortunately, the details about his sermon and the choir's song choices have been lost to history. Most of the story told here is factual, but what the Kings said and sang were creative choices I made.

When I finished writing the manuscript I set it aside, trusting that I'd find the right illustrator in due time. That I found the only illustrator right for this story is itself a testament to the power of faith. I am eternally grateful that Reverend Buckley agreed to partner with me on this project.

Illustrator's notes

Illustrating this picture book was highly personal for me during this time in our nation where there are so many concurrent factions separating the citizenry along lines of race, class and political affiliation. Dr. King and Coretta Scott King were dynamic bridge builders and truth tellers, though gone too soon, their contributions still resonate with anyone whose lives they changed. Additionally, I attended People's Baptist Church as a young child, making this story in many ways, my story.

It was exciting to create illustrations using acrylics, colored pencil, pen and ink to complement and support the author's narrative which stressed so vividly the need for people of different backgrounds to come together by learning about the "mysterious other" that comprises this great country of ours. Using a vibrant palette, I wanted to saturate the pages with a colorful kind of zing and creative energy that young readers would be attracted to while, at the same time, telling the truth about the damage done when people are separated from each other based upon the color of their skin. The images of Dr. King and Mrs. Coretta Scott King were inspired by various photographs and events in their lives. The most moving illustration for me was the drawing showing them as a young, newly married couple surrounded by the time line showing the various cities they lived in during their time together and the various accomplishments they made to teach us how to be brothers.

www.ingramcontent.com/pod-product-compliance
Lightning Source LLC
Chambersburg PA
CBHW041457040426

42447CB00004B/272